To ... 2007

Wishing you a ... holiday
Love
Wendy

Delicious

crumbles
&
cobblers

Delicious

crumbles
&
cobblers

Love Food ™ is an imprint of Parragon Books Ltd

Parragon
Queen Street House
4 Queen Street
Bath BA1 1HE, UK

Copyright © Parragon Books Ltd 2007

Love Food ™ and the accompanying heart device is a trademark of Parragon Books Ltd.

Introduction, cover text, and new recipes by Lorraine Turner
Photography by Don Last
Home economy by Christine France

ISBN 978-1-4054-9558-5
Printed in China

Notes for the reader
• This book uses imperial, metric, and US cup measurements. Follow the same units of measurement throughout; do not mix imperial and metric.
• All spoon measurements are level: teaspoons are assumed to be 5 ml, and tablespoons are assumed to be 15 ml.
• Unless otherwise stated, milk is assumed to be lowfat and eggs are medium. The times given are an approximate guide only.
• Some recipes contain nuts. If you are allergic to nuts you should avoid using them and any products containing nuts.
• Recipes using raw or very lightly cooked eggs should be avoided by infants, the elderly, pregnant women, convalescents, and anyone suffering from illness.

Contents

Introduction

Crumbles and cobblers have been around for a long time, but what exactly is the difference between them?

According to some food historians, crumbles and cobblers both originated from the pie. The pie itself can be traced back through many centuries, to the time of the ancient Egyptians. They used a primitive form of bread dough to enclose fruits and nuts, which were sweetened with honey. However, it was the ancient Greeks who first started to make pie dough with flour and water, and used it to enclose different meats. Eventually the ancient Romans adopted the pie, and later it spread to Europe.

Since then, the pie has spread around the world and has undergone many transformations, with each nation or culture adapting it to suit the circumstances and food availability of the time.

The difference between a crumble and a cobbler is that, whereas a crumble is topped with a thin, crunchy layer, a cobbler is usually topped with a thicker layer of scones. A cobbler can be either savory or sweet. In a savory cobbler the bottom layer will contain meat, fish, beans, vegetables, or a mixture of these. The topping will consist of plain or cheese-flavored scones, or scones that have been flavored with fiery or savory spices such as chile or paprika. In a sweet cobbler, the bottom layer will contain fruits, nuts, honey, and/or chocolate. The topping will comprise sweet plain scones or scones that have added ingredients such as sweet spices or dried fruits.

The crumble is an immensely useful dish for cooks on a tight budget. Thrifty cooks can use the crumble topping—a mixture of flour, sugar, and butter—as a

replacement for traditional sweet pie dough. It needs smaller quantities of the key ingredients used to make pie dough, and is therefore more economical. Its flexibility is also an attraction, because it can be used as a topping for any fruits that happen to be available at any one time.

The sugar in the crumble topping caramelizes while it is baking, creating a deliciously sweet and crunchy topping that contrasts well with the tartness of different fruits. It also pairs beautifully with chocolate and sweeteners such as honey and maple syrup. The sweetness of the topping means that sweet crumble recipes, such as fruit and chocolate, are more common, but it is also possible to make a savory version by replacing the sugar in the topping with something else, such as nuts. The Mixed Bean & Vegetable Crumble in this book is one such example, and will delight crumble enthusiasts and vegetarians alike.

Within these pages you will find some delicious cobbler recipes, from traditional favorites such as Beef Cobbler with Chile or Golden Chicken Cobbler, to innovative new interpretations on this timeless dish, such as Strawberry Cream Cobbler. Or why not try the Chocolate Cherry Crumble with Cranberries & Port, a delicious dessert to warm and delight during chilly winter nights? Whatever the occasion, and whether you are after a sweet or savory treat, there is sure to be something for everyone in this inspiring collection. Try something new today and impress your friends and family with these wonderful crumbles and cobblers!

The Classics

serves 4

2 lb/900 g tart cooking apples, peeled and sliced

10½ oz/300 g blackberries, fresh or frozen

¼ cup brown sugar

1 tsp ground cinnamon

light or heavy cream, to serve

crumble topping

⅔ cup self-rising flour

⅔ cup whole wheat all-purpose flour

½ cup butter

¼ cup raw brown sugar

apple & blackberry crumble

Preheat the oven to 400°F/200°C. Peel and core the apples and cut into chunks. Place in a bowl with the blackberries, sugar, and cinnamon and mix together, then transfer to an ovenproof baking dish.

To make the crumble topping, sift the self-rising flour into a bowl and stir in the whole wheat flour. Add the butter and rub it in with your fingertips until the mixture resembles fine breadcrumbs. Stir in the sugar.

Spread the crumble over the apples and bake in the preheated oven for 40–45 minutes, or until the apples are soft and the crumble is golden brown and crisp. Serve with cream.

serves 6

2 lb/900 g rhubarb

½ cup superfine sugar

grated rind and juice of
1 orange

cream, yogurt, or custard,
to serve

crumble topping

scant 1⅝ cups all-purpose or
whole wheat flour

½ cup butter, diced and
chilled

½ cup light brown sugar

1 tsp ground ginger

rhubarb crumble

Preheat the oven to 375°F/190°C.

Cut the rhubarb into 1-inch/2.5-cm lengths and put in an ovenproof
dish with the superfine sugar and orange rind and juice.

To make the crumble topping, sift the flour into a bowl. Rub in
the butter with your fingertips until the mixture resembles fine
breadcrumbs. Stir in the brown sugar and ginger. Spread evenly over
the fruit and press down lightly with a fork.

Bake in the center of the preheated oven for 25–30 minutes until the
crumble is golden brown.

Serve warm with cream.

serves 6

½ cup/1 tbsp butter, plus
extra for greasing

1 cup brown sugar

3 cups fresh apricots, pitted
and sliced

1 tsp ground cinnamon

crumble topping

1½ cups whole wheat flour

½ cup hazelnuts, toasted and
chopped finely

light or heavy cream, to serve

apricot crumble

Preheat the oven to 400°F/200°C.

Put 3 tablespoons of the butter and ¾ cup of the sugar in a saucepan, and melt together, stirring, over low heat. Add the apricots and cinnamon, cover the saucepan and simmer for 5 minutes.

To make the crumble topping, put the flour in a bowl and rub in the remaining butter with your fingertips until the mixture resembles fine breadcrumbs. Stir in the remaining sugar and then the hazelnuts. Remove the fruit from the heat and arrange in the bottom of an ovenproof dish. Sprinkle the crumble topping evenly over the fruit until it is covered all over. Transfer to the preheated oven and bake for about 25 minutes, until golden. Remove from the oven and serve hot with cream.

serves 6

1 lb 2 oz/500 g rhubarb

1 lb 2 oz/500 g tart cooking apples

grated rind and juice of 1 orange

½–1 tsp ground cinnamon

½ cup brown sugar

light or heavy cream, to serve

crumble topping

2 cups all-purpose flour

½ cup butter or margarine

½ cup light soft brown sugar

⅓–½ cup toasted chopped hazelnuts

2 tbsp raw brown sugar (optional)

rhubarb & orange crumble

Preheat the oven to 400°F/200°C. Cut the rhubarb into 1-inch/ 2.5-cm lengths and place in a large saucepan.

Peel, core, and slice the apples and add to the rhubarb, together with the grated orange rind and juice. Bring to a boil, reduce the heat and simmer for 2–3 minutes, until the fruit softens.

Add the cinnamon and sugar to taste and turn the mixture into an ovenproof dish, so it is not more than two-thirds full.

To make the crumble topping, sift the flour into a bowl and rub in the butter with your fingertips, until the mixture resembles fine breadcrumbs. Stir in the sugar, followed by the nuts.

Spoon the crumble mixture evenly over the fruit in the dish and smooth the top. Sprinkle with raw brown sugar, if using.

Cook in the preheated oven for 30–40 minutes, the topping is browned. Serve hot or cold with cream.

serves 4

4 apples, peeled, cored and diced

5 plums, halved, stoned and quartered

4 tbsp fresh apple juice

1 oz/25 g soft light brown sugar

light or heavy cream, to serve

crumble topping

4 oz/115 g all-purpose flour

6 tbsp margarine, diced

1 oz/25 g buckwheat flakes

1 oz/25 g rice flakes

1 oz/25 g sunflower seeds

1¾ oz/50 g soft light brown sugar

¼ tsp ground cinnamon

apple & plum crumble

Preheat the oven to 350°F/180°C. Mix the apples, plums, apple juice, and sugar together in a round pie dish.

To make the crumble topping, sift the flour into a mixing bowl and rub in the margarine with your fingertips until it resembles fine breadcrumbs. Stir in the buckwheat and rice flakes, sunflower seeds, sugar and cinnamon, then spoon the topping over the fruit in the dish.

Bake the crumble in the preheated oven for 30–35 minutes, or until the topping is lightly browned and crisp. Serve with cream.

serves 4

3 tbsp dark corn syrup

3 tbsp raw brown sugar

2 tbsp unsalted butter

2 tbsp light cream

½ tsp vanilla extract

4 large pears

vanilla ice cream, to serve

crumble topping

¾ cup self-rising flour

½ cup unsalted butter, diced

5 tbsp raw brown sugar

2 tbsp finely chopped
hazelnuts

pear & toffee crumble

Preheat the oven to 400°F/200°C. To make the crumble topping, put the flour in a large mixing bowl and rub in the butter with your fingertips, until the mixture resembles fine breadcrumbs. Stir in 4 tablespoons of the sugar and the chopped hazelnuts, then cook in the preheated oven for 5–10 minutes until heated through.

To make the toffee, put the dark corn syrup into a saucepan over low heat. Add the sugar, 1 tablespoon of the butter, and all the cream and vanilla extract, and bring gently to a boil. Simmer for 3 minutes, stirring constantly, then remove from the heat and set aside.

Put the remaining butter in a skillet and melt over low heat. Meanwhile, peel and coarsely chop the pears, then add them to the skillet and cook, stirring gently, for 3 minutes. Stir in the toffee and continue to cook, stirring, over low heat for another 3 minutes.

Transfer the pear-and-toffee mixture to an ovenproof saucepan. Arrange the crumble evenly over the top, then sprinkle over the remaining sugar. Bake in the preheated oven for 25–30 minutes, or until the crumble is golden brown. Remove from the oven and serve with vanilla ice cream.

serves 4

6 nectarines

1 oz/25 g raw brown sugar

2 tbsp sweet sherry

light or heavy cream, to serve

crumble topping

1¼ cups all-purpose flour

¼ cup raw brown sugar, plus extra for sprinkling

½ cup unsalted butter, melted

sherried nectarine crumble

Preheat the oven to 400°F/200°C. Using a sharp knife, halve the nectarines, remove and discard the pits, then cut the flesh into fairly thick slices. Put the nectarine slices into an ovenproof pan, sprinkle over the sugar and sweet sherry, then cook in the preheated oven for 5–10 minutes until heated through.

To make the crumble topping, put the flour and sugar in a large bowl, then quickly mix in the melted butter until crumbly. Carefully arrange the crumble over the nectarines in an even layer—keep your touch light or the crumble will sink into the filling and go mushy. Scatter a little more sugar over the top, then transfer to the preheated oven and bake for 25–30 minutes, or until the crumble topping is golden brown.

Remove from the oven and serve with generous spoonfuls of cream.

serves 4

14 oz/400 g gooseberries

1 tbsp honey

½ cup superfine sugar

1 tbsp orange juice

1 tbsp grated orange zest

6 tbsp water

zest, to decorate

vanilla- or orange-flavored
ice cream, to serve

crumble topping

¾ cup self-rising flour

½ cup unsalted butter, diced

5 tbsp raw brown sugar

1¾ oz/50 g pistachios,
finely chopped

gooseberry & pistachio crumble

Preheat the oven to 400°F/200°C. Put the gooseberries in an ovenproof saucepan, pour over the honey, and cook in the preheated oven for 5–10 minutes until heated through.

Put the superfine sugar, orange juice, orange zest, and water in a small saucepan, then bring to a boil, stirring, over medium heat. Reduce the heat and simmer for 5 minutes, then remove from the heat and let cool.

Meanwhile, to make the crumble topping, put the flour in a bowl, then rub in the butter with your fingertips, until the mixture resembles fine breadcrumbs. Now stir in 4 tablespoons of the raw brown sugar and the pistachios.

Pour the cooled orange syrup over the gooseberries, then lightly sprinkle over the crumble mixture in an even layer. Do not press the crumble into the syrup or it will become mushy. Sprinkle over the remaining raw brown sugar.

Bake in the preheated oven for 25–30 minutes or until the crumble topping is golden brown. Remove from the oven and serve with vanilla- or orange-flavored ice cream.

serves 4

6 peaches

2 tbsp raw brown sugar

2 tbsp orange juice

light or heavy cream, to serve

crumble topping

¾ cup self-rising flour

½ cup unsalted butter, diced

5 tbsp raw brown sugar

3 tbsp finely chopped hazelnuts

peach & orange crumble

Preheat the oven to 400°F/200°C. Using a sharp knife, halve the peaches, remove and discard the pits, then cut the flesh into fairly thick slices. Put the peach slices into an ovenproof saucepan, sprinkle over the sugar and orange juice, then cook in the preheated oven for 5–10 minutes until heated through.

To make the crumble topping, put the flour in a large bowl, then rub in the butter with your fingertips, until the mixture resembles fine breadcrumbs. Stir in 4 tablespoons of the sugar and the hazelnuts. Carefully arrange the crumble over the peaches in an even layer—keep your touch light or the crumble will sink into the filling and go mushy. Scatter the remaining sugar over the top, then transfer to the preheated oven and bake for 25–30 minutes, or until the crumble topping` is golden brown.

Remove from the oven and serve with cream.

serves 4

4 just-ripe bananas (not too ripe or they will be too mushy for this dish)

2 tbsp rum

fine strips of lime zest, to decorate

vanilla ice cream, to serve

crumble topping

½ cup self-rising flour

zest of 1 lime, finely grated

½ cup unsalted butter, diced

5 tbsp raw brown sugar

1¾ oz/50 g dry unsweetened coconut

baked banana crumble with rum & lime

Preheat the oven to 400°F/200°C. To make the crumble topping, put the flour and grated lime zest in a bowl, then rub in the butter with your fingertips, until the mixture resembles fine breadcrumbs. Stir in 4 tablespoons of the raw brown sugar and the coconut and set aside.

Slice the bananas lengthwise and arrange them in an even layer in the bottom of an ovenproof saucepan. Pour over the rum, then lightly sprinkle over the crumble topping to cover the bananas. Do not press the mixture down or the bananas and crumble will go mushy. Sprinkle the remaining sugar over the top, then transfer to the preheated oven and bake for 20–25 minutes, or until the crumble is golden brown.

Remove from the oven, decorate with strips of lime zest, and serve with vanilla ice cream.

Contemporary Twists

serves 4

butter, for greasing

14 oz/400 g canned apricots, in natural juice

1 lb/450 g tart cooking apples, peeled and sliced thickly

crumble topping

6 tbsp butter

¾ cup all-purpose flour

⅔ cup rolled oats

4 tbsp superfine sugar

⅔ cup semisweet or milk chocolate chips

light or heavy cream, to serve

chocolate fruit crumble

Preheat the oven to 350°F/180°C. Lightly grease an ovenproof dish with a little butter.

Drain the apricots, reserving 4 tablespoons of the juice. Place the apples and apricots in the prepared ovenproof dish with the reserved apricot juice and toss to mix.

To make the crumble topping, sift the flour into a bowl and rub in the butter with your fingertips, until the mixture resembles fine breadcrumbs. Stir in the rolled oats, sugar, and chocolate chips.

Sprinkle the crumble mixture over the apples and apricots and smooth the top coarsely. Do not press the crumble into the fruit.

Bake in the preheated oven for 40–45 minutes, or until the topping is golden. Serve hot or cold with cream.

serves 4

2 mangoes, sliced

1 papaya, seeded and sliced

8 oz/225 g fresh pineapple, cubed

1½ tsp ground ginger

7 tbsp margarine

½ cup brown sugar

crumble topping

1½ cups all-purpose flour

⅔ cup dry unsweetened coconut, plus extra to decorate

light or heavy cream, to serve

tropical fruit crumble

Preheat the oven to 350°F/180°C. Place the fruit in a saucepan with ½ teaspoon of the ground ginger, 2 tablespoons of the margarine, and 4 tablespoons of the sugar. Cook over low heat for 10 minutes until the fruit softens. Spoon the fruit into the bottom of a shallow ovenproof dish.

To make the crumble topping, combine the flour and remaining ginger. Rub in the remaining margarine until the mixture resembles fine breadcrumbs. Stir in the remaining sugar and the coconut and spoon over the fruit to cover completely.

Cook the crumble in the preheated oven for about 40 minutes or until the top is crisp. Decorate with a sprinkling of dry unsweetened coconut and serve immediately with cream.

serves 4

3 large, ripe cooking apples

3 large, ripe pears

1–2 tbsp lemon juice

½ cup unsalted butter

½ cup maple syrup

1 tsp almond extract

1 tsp almond-flavored liqueur, such as Amaretto (optional)

whole or chopped almonds, to decorate

light or heavy cream, to serve

crumble topping

¾ cup self-rising flour

½ cup unsalted butter, diced

5 tbsp raw brown sugar

1¾ oz/50 g almonds, finely chopped

caramelized apple & pear crumble

Preheat the oven to 375°F/190°C. Peel and core the apples and pears, then cut them into small chunks. Brush the chunks with a little lemon juice to prevent discoloration.

Melt the butter in a skillet over medium-low heat, add the apples and pears, maple syrup, and almond extract, and almond liqueur if using. Cook the fruit for 5–7 minutes until softened, then remove from the heat and arrange the fruit and juices evenly in the bottom of an ovenproof saucepan.

Meanwhile, to make the crumble topping, put the flour in a bowl, then rub in the butter with your fingertips, until the mixture resembles fine breadcrumbs. Now stir in 4 tablespoons of the raw brown sugar and the almonds. Lightly sprinkle the crumble mixture over the fruit in an even layer. Do not press the crumble into the syrup or it will become mushy. Sprinkle over the remaining raw brown sugar and decorate with whole or chopped almonds.

Bake in the preheated oven for 20–25 minutes or until the crumble topping is golden brown. Remove from the oven and serve with cream.

serves 4

6 oz/175 g cherries, pitted

5½ oz/150 g cranberries

3 tbsp raw brown sugar

6 tbsp port

light or heavy cream, to serve

crumble topping

¾ cup self-rising flour

½ cup unsalted butter, diced

5 tbsp raw brown sugar

2 tbsp finely chopped mixed nuts

1¾ oz/50 g semisweet chocolate, finely chopped

chocolate cherry crumble with cranberries & port

Preheat the oven to 400°F/200°C. To make the crumble topping, put the flour in a large mixing bowl, then rub in the butter with your fingertips until the mixture resembles fine breadcrumbs. Stir in 4 tablespoons of the sugar and the chopped mixed nuts, then stir in the chopped chocolate and set aside.

To make the filling, put the cherries, cranberries, sugar, and port into a saucepan and stir gently over low heat for 3 minutes. Transfer the fruit and juices to an ovenproof saucepan and sprinkle over the crumble topping. Scatter over the remaining sugar. Bake in the preheated oven for 10–15 minutes, or until the crumble topping is golden brown. Remove from the oven and serve with cream.

makes 12

2 cups all-purpose flour

2 tsp baking powder

¼ tsp baking soda

¼ tsp salt

¾ cup milk

2 medium eggs

⅔ cup unsalted butter, melted

4 oz/115 g fresh cranberries, coarsely chopped

2¾ oz/75 g mixed nuts, chopped

1 cup raw brown sugar

streusel topping

⅔ cup self-rising flour

1 tsp mixed spice

2 tbsp unsalted butter, diced

½ cup raw brown sugar

4 tbsp chopped mixed nuts

cranberry streusel muffins

Preheat the oven to 375°F/190°C. Line a 12-cup muffin saucepan with paper cases.

Sift the flour, baking powder, baking soda, and salt into a large mixing bowl. Make a well in the center and add the milk, eggs, and melted butter. Stir together gently until just combined. Do not overstir—the mixture should still be a little lumpy.

Add the cranberries, mixed nuts, and sugar, and again stir lightly, just enough to incorporate the fruit and nuts evenly into the batter. Distribute the batter evenly between the paper cases.

To make the streusel topping, put the flour and mixed spice in a bowl, then use your fingertips to rub in the butter until crumbly. Stir in the raw brown sugar and the mixed nuts. At this stage you may need to add a little cold water to make the mixture stick loosely together. Arrange the streusel topping on top of the muffins, then bake in the preheated oven for 20–25 minutes, until golden brown on top. To test whether they are cooked, insert a toothpick into the center of a muffin. If it comes out clean, the muffins are cooked. If not, return them to the oven for a few more minutes until cooked.

serves 4

2¼ oz/60 g unsweetened cocoa

1 cup water

⅔ cup superfine sugar

2 tbsp unsalted butter, diced

4 large cooking apples

crumble topping

¾ cup self-rising flour

1 tbsp unsweetened cocoa

½ cup unsalted butter, diced

5 tbsp dark brown sugar

2 tbsp finely chopped pecans

1¾ oz/50 g semisweet chocolate, finely chopped

deep chocolate crumble

Preheat the oven to 350°F/180°C. To make the crumble topping, put the flour and cocoa in a large mixing bowl, then rub in the butter with your fingertips until the mixture resembles fine breadcrumbs. Stir in 4 tablespoons of the sugar and the chopped pecans, then stir in the chopped chocolate and set aside.

To make the filling, put the cocoa, water, and superfine sugar in a small saucepan and cook, stirring, over low heat for 3 minutes. Add the diced butter and return to a simmer, stirring constantly, then remove from the heat.

Peel and slice the apples, then spread them evenly in the bottom of an ovenproof saucepan (this has to be done quickly to prevent the apples from discoloring). Pour over half of the chocolate sauce, then sprinkle over the crumble topping. Scatter over the remaining sugar. Bake in the preheated oven for about 20–25 minutes, or until the crumble topping is cooked. Just before the end of the cooking time, return the remaining chocolate sauce to the hob and warm gently. Remove the crumble from the oven and serve with the warmed chocolate sauce.

serves 4

8 firm but ripe plums

1 oz/25 g raw brown sugar

light or heavy cream, to serve

crumble topping

1¼ cups all-purpose flour

1¼ cup raw brown sugar, plus
extra for sprinkling

½ cup unsalted butter, melted

1¾ oz/50 g hazelnuts,
chopped

mini plum crumbles

Preheat the oven to 350°F/180°C. Using a sharp knife, halve the plums, remove and discard the pits, then cut the flesh into fairly thick slices. Divide the plum slices between 4 ovenproof ramekins, sprinkle over the sugar, then cook in the preheated oven for 5–10 minutes until heated through.

To make the crumble topping, put the flour and sugar in a large bowl, then mix in half the melted butter. Stir in the chopped nuts, then quickly mix in the remaining butter until crumbly. Carefully arrange the crumble over the plums in an even layer—keep your touch light or the crumble will sink into the filling and go mushy. Scatter a little more sugar over the top, then transfer to the preheated oven and bake for 25 minutes, or until the crumble topping is golden brown.

Remove from the oven and serve with cream.

serves 8

pie dough

1¼ cups all-purpose flour

1 tsp baking powder

½ cup unsalted butter,
cut into small pieces

¼ cup superfine sugar

1 egg yolk

1–2 tsp cold water

filling

⅔ cup heavy cream

⅔ cup milk

8 oz/225 g semisweet
chocolate, chopped

2 eggs

crumble topping

½ cup packed brown sugar

¾ cup toasted pecans

4 oz/115 g semisweet chocolate

3 oz/85 g amaretti cookies

1 tsp unsweetened cocoa

chocolate crumble pie

To make the pie dough, sift the flour and baking powder into a large bowl, rub in the butter, and stir in the sugar, then add the egg and a little water to bring the dough together. Turn the dough out, and knead briefly. Wrap the dough and let chill in the refrigerator for 30 minutes.

Preheat the oven to 375°F/190°C. Roll out the pie dough and use to line a 9-inch/23-cm loose-bottom tart saucepan. Prick the pastry shell with a fork. Line with parchment paper and fill with dried beans. Bake in the oven for 15 minutes. Remove from the oven and take out the paper and beans. Reduce the oven temperature to 350°F/180°C.

Bring the cream and milk to a boil in a saucepan, remove from the heat, and add the chocolate. Stir until melted and smooth. Beat the eggs and add to the chocolate mixture, mix thoroughly, and pour into the shell. Bake for 15 minutes, remove from the oven, and let rest for 1 hour.

When you are ready to serve the pie, place the topping ingredients in the food processor and pulse to chop. (If you do not have a processor, place the sugar in a large bowl, chop the nuts and chocolate with a large knife, and crush the cookies, then add to the bowl with the cocoa and mix well.) Sprinkle over the pie, then serve it in slices.

serves 6

4 lb/1.8 kg sweet pumpkin

4 tbsp cold unsalted butter, in small pieces, plus extra for greasing

1 cup all-purpose flour, plus extra for dusting

¼ tsp baking powder

1½ tsp ground cinnamon

¾ tsp ground nutmeg

¾ tsp ground cloves

1 tsp salt

¼ cup superfine sugar

3 eggs

1¾ cups sweetened condensed milk

½ tsp vanilla extract

1 tbsp raw sugar

streusel topping

2 tbsp all-purpose flour

4 tbsp raw sugar

1 tsp ground cinnamon

2 tbsp cold unsalted butter, in small pieces

⅔ cup shelled pecans, chopped

⅔ cup shelled walnuts, chopped

sweet pumpkin pie

Preheat the oven to 375°F/190°C. Halve the pumpkin and remove the seeds, stem, and stringy insides. Place the pumpkin halves, face down, in a shallow baking saucepan and cover with foil. Bake in the preheated oven for 1½ hours, then remove from the oven and let cool. Scoop out the flesh and mash with a potato masher. Drain away any excess liquid. Cover with plastic wrap and let chill.

To make the pie dough, first grease a 9-inch/23-cm round pie dish with butter. Sift the flour and baking powder into a large bowl. Stir in ½ tsp cinnamon, ¼ tsp nutmeg, ¼ tsp cloves, ½ tsp salt, and all the superfine sugar. Rub in the butter with the fingertips until the mixture resembles fine breadcrumbs, then make a well in the center. Lightly beat 1 egg and pour it into the well. Mix together with a wooden spoon, then use your hands to shape the dough into a ball. Place it on a clean counter lightly dusted with flour, and roll out to a circle large enough to line the pie dish. Use it to line the dish, then trim the edge. Cover the dish with plastic wrap and let chill in the refrigerator for 30 minutes.

Preheat the oven to 425°F/220°C. To make the filling, place the pumpkin purée in a large bowl, then stir in the condensed milk and remaining eggs. Add the remaining spices and salt, then stir in the vanilla extract and raw sugar. Pour into the pastry shell and bake for 15 minutes.

Meanwhile, make the topping. Combine the flour, sugar, and cinnamon in a bowl, rub in the butter with your fingertips until the mixture resembles fine breadcrumbs, then stir in the nuts. Remove the pie from the oven and reduce the heat to 350°F/180°C. Sprinkle the topping over the pie, then bake for an additional 35 minutes. Remove from the oven and serve hot or cold.

serves 4

1 large onion, peeled and chopped

4$^1/_2$ oz/125 g canned red kidney beans (drained weight)

4$^1/_2$ oz/125 g canned lima beans (drained weight)

4$^1/_2$ oz/125 g canned chickpeas (drained weight)

2 zucchini, coarsely chopped

2 large carrots, coarsely chopped

4 tomatoes, peeled and coarsely chopped

2 celery stalks, trimmed and chopped

1$^1/_4$ cups vegetable stock

2 tbsp tomato paste

salt and pepper

crumble topping

1$^3/_4$ cups whole wheat breadcrumbs

1 oz/25 g hazelnuts, very finely chopped

1 heaping tbsp chopped fresh parsley

1 cup grated Cheddar cheese

mixed bean & vegetable crumble

Preheat the oven to 350°F/180°C. Put the onion, kidney beans, lima beans, chickpeas, zucchini, carrots, tomatoes, and celery in a large ovenproof pan. Mix together the stock and tomato paste and pour over the vegetables. Season to taste with salt and pepper. Transfer to the preheated oven and bake for 15 minutes.

Meanwhile, to make the crumble topping, put the breadcrumbs in a large bowl, add the hazelnuts, chopped parsley, and grated cheese, and mix together well.

Remove the vegetables from the oven and carefully sprinkle over the crumble topping. Do not press it down or it will sink into the vegetables and go mushy. Return to the oven and bake for 30 minutes, or until the crumble topping is golden brown. Remove from the oven and serve hot.

3

Cobblers & Beyond

serves 6

2 lb/900 g fresh berries and currants, such as blackberries, blueberries, raspberries, red currants, and black currants

$^1/_2$ cup superfine sugar

2 tbsp cornstarch

light or heavy cream, to serve

cobbler topping

1$^1/_3$ cups all-purpose flour

2 tsp baking powder

pinch of salt

4 tbsp unsalted butter, diced and chilled

2 tbsp superfine sugar

$^3/_4$ cup buttermilk

1 tbsp raw brown sugar

fruit cobbler

Preheat the oven to 400°F/200°C. Pick over the fruit, then mix with the superfine sugar and cornstarch and put in a 10-inch/25-cm shallow, ovenproof dish.

To make the cobbler topping, sift the flour, baking powder, and salt into a large bowl. Rub in the butter with your fingertips until the mixture resembles fine breadcrumbs, then stir in the superfine sugar. Pour in the buttermilk and mix to a soft dough.

Drop spoonfuls of the dough on top of the fruit roughly, so that it doesn't completely cover the fruit. Sprinkle with the raw brown sugar and bake in the preheated oven for 25–30 minutes, or until the crust is golden and the fruit is tender.

Remove from the oven and let stand for a few minutes before serving with cream.

serves 4–6

6 peaches, peeled and sliced

4 tbsp superfine sugar

$1/2$ tbsp lemon juice

$1^1/2$ tsp cornstarch

$1/2$ tsp almond or vanilla extract

vanilla or butter pecan ice cream, to serve

cobbler topping

$1^1/4$ cups all-purpose flour

$1/2$ cup superfine sugar

$1^1/2$ tsp baking powder

$1/2$ tsp salt

6 tbsp butter, diced

1 egg

5–6 tbsp milk

peach cobbler

Preheat the oven to 425°F/220°C. Put the peaches into an ovenproof dish that is also suitable for serving. Add the sugar, lemon juice, cornstarch, and almond extract and toss together. Bake the peaches in the oven for 20 minutes.

Meanwhile, to make the cobbler topping, sift the flour, all but 2 tablespoons of the sugar, the baking powder, and salt into a bowl. Rub in the butter with your fingertips until the mixture resembles fine breadcrumbs. Combine the egg and 5 tablespoons of the milk in a pitcher and mix into the dry ingredients with a fork until a soft, sticky dough forms. If the dough seems dry, stir in the extra tablespoon of milk.

Reduce the oven temperature to 400°F/200°C. Remove the peaches from the oven and drop spoonfuls of the topping over the surface, without smoothing. Sprinkle with the remaining sugar, return to the oven, and bake for an additional 15 minutes, or until the topping is golden brown and firm—the topping will spread as it cooks. Serve hot or at room temperature with ice cream on the side.

serves 4

1 lb 12 oz/800 g strawberries, hulled and halved

$1/4$ cup superfine sugar

whipped heavy cream

cobbler topping

$1^{1}/_{2}$ cups self-rising flour, plus extra for dusting

pinch of salt

3 tbsp butter

2 tbsp superfine sugar

1 egg, beaten

1 oz/25 g golden raisins

1 oz/25 g raisins

5 tbsp milk, plus extra for glazing

strawberry cream cobbler

Preheat the oven to 400°F/200°C. Arrange the strawberries evenly in the bottom of an ovenproof saucepan, then sprinkle over the sugar and cook in the preheated oven for 5–10 minutes until heated through.

To make the cobbler topping, sift the flour and salt into a large mixing bowl. Rub in the butter with your fingertips until the mixture resembles fine breadcrumbs, then stir in the sugar. Add the beaten egg, then the golden raisins and raisins and mix lightly until incorporated. Stir in enough of the milk to make a smooth dough. Transfer to a clean, lightly floured board, knead lightly, then roll out to a thickness of about $1/2$ inch/1 cm. Cut out circles using a 2-inch/5-cm cookie cutter. Arrange the dough circles over the strawberries, then brush the tops with a little milk.

Bake in the preheated oven for 25–30 minutes, or until the cobbler topping has risen and is lightly golden. Remove from the oven and serve with whipped heavy cream.

serves 4

4 peaches, halved and pitted

4 nectarines, halved and pitted

2 tbsp almond liqueur, such as Amaretto

¼ cup superfine sugar

light or heavy cream, to serve

cobbler topping

1½ cups self-rising flour, plus extra for dusting

pinch of salt

3 tbsp butter

2 tbsp superfine sugar

1 egg, beaten

5 tbsp milk, plus extra for glazing

1 oz/25 g slivered almonds

peach & nectarine cobbler with almond liqueur

Preheat the oven to 400°F/200°C. Arrange the peaches and nectarines evenly in the bottom of an ovenproof saucepan, then sprinkle over the almond liqueur and the sugar and cook in the preheated oven for 5–10 minutes until heated through.

To make the cobbler topping, sift the flour and salt into a large mixing bowl. Rub in the butter with your fingertips until the mixture resembles fine breadcrumbs, then mix in the sugar, followed by the beaten egg. Stir in enough of the milk to make a smooth dough. Transfer to a clean, lightly floured board, knead lightly, then roll out to a thickness of about ½ inch/1 cm. Cut out circles using a 2-inch/5-cm cookie cutter. Arrange the dough circles over the fruit, brush the tops with a little milk, then scatter over the slivered almonds.

Bake in the preheated oven for 25–30 minutes, or until the cobbler topping has risen and is lightly golden. Remove from the oven and serve with cream.

serves 4

2 tbsp all-purpose flour

4 skinless, boneless chicken breasts, cut into bite-size chunks

2 tbsp butter

2 tbsp olive oil

1 large leek, trimmed and sliced

2 scallions, trimmed and chopped

1 garlic clove, crushed

2 carrots, peeled and chopped

1 orange bell pepper, seeded and chopped

1 tbsp tomato paste

1/2 tsp ground turmeric

3/4 cup white wine

3/4 cup chicken stock

1 bay leaf

salt and pepper

cobbler topping

1 1/4 cups self-rising flour, plus extra for dusting

2 level tsp baking powder

1/2 tsp ground turmeric

3 tbsp butter

4–5 tbsp milk

salt

golden chicken cobbler

Preheat the oven to 350°F/180°C. Put the flour in a bowl, season with salt and pepper, then add the chicken chunks and toss in the flour to coat. Melt the butter with the oil in a large flameproof casserole, add the chicken, and cook, stirring, until the chicken is golden all over. Lift out with a slotted spoon, transfer to a plate, and set aside.

Add the leek, scallions, and garlic to the casserole and cook over medium heat, stirring, for 2 minutes until softened. Add the carrots and orange bell pepper and cook for another 2 minutes, then stir in the remaining seasoned flour, the tomato paste, and the turmeric. Pour in the wine and stock, bring to a boil, then reduce the heat and cook over low heat, stirring, until thickened. Return the chicken to the saucepan, add the bay leaf, cover, then bake in the preheated oven for 30 minutes.

Meanwhile, to make the cobbler topping, sift the flour, baking powder, turmeric, and a pinch of salt into a large mixing bowl. Rub in the butter until the mixture resembles fine breadcrumbs, then stir in enough of the milk to make a smooth dough. Transfer to a clean, lightly floured board, knead lightly, then roll out to a thickness of about 1/2 inch/1 cm. Cut out circles using a 2-inch/5-cm cookie cutter.

Remove the casserole from the oven, remove and discard the bay leaf, and adjust the seasoning. Arrange the dough circles over the top, then return to the oven and bake for another 30 minutes, or until the cobbler topping has risen and is lightly golden. Remove from the oven and serve hot.

serves 4

2 tbsp butter

2 large leeks, trimmed and sliced

5$\frac{1}{2}$ oz/150 g white mushrooms, sliced

2 zucchini, sliced

4 large tomatoes, peeled and chopped

1 tbsp chopped fresh dill

$\frac{1}{2}$ cup white wine

$\frac{3}{4}$ cup fish stock

4 tsp cornstarch

8 oz/225 g cod, cut into bite-size chunks

8 oz/225 g haddock, cut into bite-size chunks

salt and pepper

cobbler topping

1$\frac{1}{4}$ cups self-rising flour, plus extra for dusting

2 level tsp baking powder

1 tbsp chopped fresh dill

3 tbsp butter

4–5 tbsp milk

salt

mixed fish cobbler with dill

Preheat the oven to 400°F/200°C. Melt the butter in a large flameproof casserole over low heat. Add the leeks and cook, stirring, for 2 minutes until slightly softened. Add the mushrooms, zucchini, tomatoes, and dill, and cook, stirring, for another 3 minutes.

Stir in the white wine and stock, bring to a boil, then reduce the heat to a simmer. Mix the cornstarch with a little water to form a paste, then stir it into the casserole. Cook, stirring constantly, until thickened, then season with salt and pepper and remove from the heat.

To make the cobbler topping, sift the flour, baking powder, and a pinch of salt into a large mixing bowl. Stir in the dill, then rub in the butter with your fingertips until the mixture resembles fine breadcrumbs. Stir in enough of the milk to make a smooth dough. Transfer to a clean, lightly floured board, knead lightly, then roll out to a thickness of about $\frac{1}{2}$ inch/1 cm. Cut out circles using a 2-inch/5-cm cookie cutter.

Add the cod and haddock to the casserole and stir gently to mix. Arrange the dough circles over the top, then return to the oven and bake for another 30 minutes, or until the cobbler topping has risen and is lightly golden. Remove from the oven and serve hot.

serves 4

1 tbsp olive oil

1 garlic clove, crushed

8 small onions, halved

2 celery stalks, sliced

8 oz/225 g rutabaga, chopped

2 carrots, sliced

$^1/_2$ small cauliflower, broken into florets

3$^1/_4$ cups sliced mushrooms

14 oz/400 g canned chopped tomatoes

$^1/_4$ cup red lentils, rinsed

2 tbsp cornstarch

3–4 tbsp water

1$^1/_4$ cups vegetable stock

2 tsp Tabasco sauce

2 tsp chopped fresh oregano

cobbler topping

2 cups self-rising flour

4 tbsp butter

1 cup grated sharp Cheddar cheese

2 tsp chopped fresh oregano

1 egg, lightly beaten

$^2/_3$ cup milk

salt

winter vegetable cobbler

Heat the oil and cook the garlic and onions for 5 minutes. Add the celery, rutabaga, carrots, and cauliflower and cook for 2–3 minutes. Add the mushrooms, tomatoes, and lentils. Mix the cornstarch and water and stir into the saucepan with the stock, Tabasco, and oregano.

Transfer to a casserole, cover, and bake in a preheated oven, 350°F/180°C, for 20 minutes.

To make the cobbler topping, sift the flour with a pinch of salt into a bowl. Rub in the butter with your fingertips, then stir in most of the cheese and the chopped oregano. Beat the egg with the milk and add enough to the dry ingredients to make a soft dough. Knead lightly, roll out to $^1/_2$ inch/1 cm thick and cut into 2-inch/5-cm rounds.

Remove the casserole from the oven and increase the temperature to 400°F/200°C. Arrange the scones around the edge of the casserole, brush with the remaining egg and milk, and sprinkle with the reserved cheese. Cook for a further 10–12 minutes. Serve.

serves 6–8

butter, for greasing

1 lb/450 g black cherries, pitted

2 tbsp golden granulated sugar

3 eggs

$^1/_4$ cup golden superfine sugar

$^1/_2$ cup self-rising flour

$^1/_4$ cup unsweetened cocoa

$^3/_4$ cup heavy cream

$1^1/_4$ cups milk

2 tbsp kirsch (optional)

light or heavy cream, to serve

cherry & chocolate clafoutis

Preheat the oven to 375°F/190°C. Lightly butter a 9-inch/23-cm ovenproof tart dish. Arrange the cherries in the dish, sprinkle with the granulated sugar, and set aside.

Put the eggs and superfine sugar in a bowl and whisk together until light and frothy. Sift the flour and unsweetened cocoa onto a plate and add, all at once, to the egg mixture. Beat in thoroughly, then whisk in the cream followed by the milk and kirsch, if using. Pour the batter over the cherries.

Bake in the oven for 50–60 minutes, until slightly risen and set in the center. Serve warm, with cream.

serves 4

2 tbsp butter, for greasing

$1/2$ cup superfine sugar

3 eggs

$1/2$ cup all-purpose flour

1 cup light cream

$1/2$ tsp ground cinnamon

1 lb/450 g blueberries

confectioners' sugar,
to decorate

light or heavy cream, to serve

blueberry clafoutis

Preheat the oven to 350°F/180°C.

Put the butter in a bowl with the sugar and cream together until fluffy. Add the eggs and beat together well. Mix in the flour, then gradually stir in the cream followed by the cinnamon. Continue to stir until smooth.

Arrange the blueberries in the bottom of the prepared dish, then pour over the cream batter. Transfer to the preheated oven and bake for about 30 minutes, or until puffed and golden.

Remove from the oven, dust with confectioners' sugar, and serve with cream.

serves 8

pie dough

6 tbsp butter, cut into small pieces, plus extra for greasing

1¼ cups all-purpose flour

1 tbsp water

1 egg, separated

sugar lumps, crushed, for sprinkling

light or heavy cream, to serve

filling

1 lb 5 oz/600 g prepared fruit (plums, rhubarb, or gooseberries)

⅓ cup packed brown sugar

1 tbsp ground ginger

one-roll fruit pie

Grease a large cookie sheet with a little butter and set aside until required.

To make the pie dough, place the flour and butter in a mixing bowl and rub in the butter with your fingertips, until the mixture resembles fine breadcrumbs. Add the water and work the mixture together until a soft dough has formed. Form into a ball. Wrap the dough and let chill in the refrigerator for 30 minutes. Preheat the oven to 400°F/200°C. Roll out the chilled dough to a circle about 14 inches/35 cm in diameter.

Transfer the dough circle to the center of the prepared cookie sheet. Lightly beat the egg yolk, then brush the dough with it.

To make the filling, mix the fruit with the brown sugar and ground ginger. Pile it into the center of the dough.

Turn in the edges of the dough circle all the way around. Lightly beat the egg white, then brush the surface of the dough with it, and sprinkle with the crushed sugar lumps.

Bake in the preheated oven for 35 minutes, or until golden brown. Serve warm with cream.

4

Nice 'n' Spicy

serves 4

10 firm but ripe apricots,
pitted and halved

1 oz/25 g raw brown sugar

$^{1}/_{2}$ tsp ground ginger

1 tbsp orange juice

grated zest of 1 orange

1 tbsp orange-flavored
liqueur, such as Cointreau

chopped pistachios,
to decorate

light or heavy cream, to serve

crumble topping

$^{3}/_{4}$ cup self-rising flour

$^{1}/_{2}$ tsp ground ginger

$^{1}/_{2}$ cup unsalted butter, diced

5 tbsp raw brown sugar

1$^{3}/_{4}$ oz/50 g pistachios,
finely chopped

apricot & ginger crumble with orange liqueur

Preheat the oven to 400°F/200°C. Put the apricots in the bottom of an ovenproof saucepan, sprinkle over the sugar, ginger, orange juice and zest, and the orange-flavored liqueur, then cook in the preheated oven for 5–10 minutes until heated through.

Meanwhile, to make the crumble topping, put the flour and ginger in a bowl, then rub in the butter with your fingertips until the mixture resembles fine breadcrumbs. Now stir in 4 tablespoons of the raw brown sugar and the pistachios. Lightly sprinkle the crumble mixture over the fruit in an even layer. Do not press the crumble into the fruit or it will become mushy. Sprinkle over the remaining raw brown sugar and decorate with chopped pistachios.

Bake in the preheated oven for 25–30 minutes or until the crumble topping is golden brown. Remove from the oven and serve with cream.

serves 4

8 oz/225 g raisins

8 oz/225 g dried figs, chopped

3 cups water

3 tbsp raw brown sugar

grated zest and juice of
1 orange

½ tsp ground cloves, or
to taste

vanilla- or orange-flavored
ice cream, to serve

crumble topping

1¼ cups all-purpose flour

¼ cup raw brown sugar, plus
extra for sprinkling

½ cup unsalted butter, melted

1¾ oz/50 g hazelnuts,
chopped

sweet fig & raisin crumble

Put the raisins and figs in a large bowl, cover with the water, and let soak overnight or for at least 8 hours.

Preheat the oven to 350°F/180°C. Drain the figs and raisins but reserve the soaking liquid. Put the fruit in a large saucepan with the sugar and 2½ cups of the soaking liquid. Bring to a boil, then reduce the heat and simmer for about 10 minutes, or until the fruit has softened.

Meanwhile, to make the crumble topping, put the flour and sugar in a large bowl, then mix in half the melted butter. Stir in the chopped nuts, then quickly mix in the remaining butter until crumbly.

Remove the fruit from the heat, stir in the orange zest and juice, and the ground cloves, then carefully pour into an ovenproof pan. Carefully arrange the crumble over the fruit in an even layer—keep your touch light or the crumble will sink into the filling and go mushy. Scatter a little more sugar over the top, then transfer to the preheated oven and bake for 25 minutes, or until the crumble topping is golden brown.

Remove from the oven and serve with vanilla- or orange-flavored ice cream.

serves 4

8 oz/225 g prunes, chopped

8 oz/225 g golden raisins

3 cups water

3 tbsp raw brown sugar

1 tsp mixed spice

1 tbsp dark rum (optional)

light or heavy cream, to serve

crumble topping

³⁄₄ cup self-rising flour

¹⁄₂ tsp mixed spice

¹⁄₂ cup unsalted butter, diced

5 tbsp raw brown sugar

prune & golden raisin crumble with mixed spices

Put the prunes and golden raisins in a large bowl, cover with the water, and let soak overnight or for at least 8 hours.

Preheat the oven to 350°F/180°C. Drain the fruit but reserve the soaking liquid. Put the fruit in a large saucepan with the sugar and 2¹⁄₂ cups of the soaking liquid. Bring to a boil, then reduce the heat and simmer for about 10 minutes, or until the fruit has softened.

Meanwhile, to make the crumble topping, put the flour and mixed spice in a bowl, then rub in the butter with your fingertips until the mixture resembles fine breadcrumbs. Now stir in 4 tablespoons of the raw brown sugar.

Remove the fruit from the heat, stir in the mixed spice, and the rum, if using, then pour into an ovenproof saucepan. Carefully arrange the crumble over the fruit in an even layer—keep your touch light or the crumble will sink into the filling and go mushy. Scatter the remaining sugar over the top, then transfer to the preheated oven and bake for 25 minutes, or until the crumble topping is golden brown.

Remove from the oven and serve with cream.

serves 4

8 firm but ripe plums

1 oz/25 g raw brown sugar

$^1/_2$ tsp ground ginger

grated zest of 1 lemon

pieces of preserved ginger,
to decorate

light or heavy cream, to serve

crumble topping

1$^1/_4$ cups all-purpose flour

$^1/_2$ tsp ground ginger

$^1/_4$ cup raw brown sugar, plus
extra for sprinkling

$^1/_2$ cup unsalted butter,
melted

plum crumble with lemon & ginger

Preheat the oven to 400°F/200°C. Using a sharp knife, halve the plums, remove and discard the pits, then cut the flesh into fairly thick slices. Arrange the plum slices in an ovenproof saucepan, sprinkle over the sugar, ground ginger, and lemon zest, then cook in the preheated oven for 5–10 minutes until heated through.

To make the crumble topping, put the flour, ground ginger, and sugar in a large bowl, then mix in the melted butter until crumbly. Carefully arrange the crumble over the plums in an even layer—keep your touch light or the crumble will sink into the filling and go mushy. Scatter a little more sugar over the top, then transfer to the preheated oven and bake for 25–30 minutes, or until the crumble topping is golden brown.

Remove from the oven and decorate with the preserved ginger. Serve with cream.

serves 4

6 large, firm peaches

$\frac{1}{4}$ cup unsalted butter

$\frac{1}{2}$ tsp ground star anise

2 tbsp superfine sugar

$\frac{1}{2}$ cup water

2 tbsp kirsch

vanilla- or peach-flavored ice cream, to serve

crumble topping

$\frac{3}{4}$ cup self-rising flour

$\frac{1}{2}$ tsp ground cinnamon

$\frac{1}{2}$ cup unsalted butter, diced

5 tbsp raw brown sugar

$1\frac{3}{4}$ oz/50 g cashews, finely chopped

roasted peach crumble with star anise

Preheat the oven to 375°F/190°C. Using a sharp knife, halve the peaches and remove the pits. Bring a saucepan of water to a boil, add the peach halves, then cook for about 3 minutes until the skins are wrinkled. Remove from the heat, lift out the peaches, and let cool slightly.

Melt the butter in a small saucepan, add the star anise, and cook, stirring for 30 seconds. Add the superfine sugar and the water and cook gently, stirring, until beginning to caramelize. Stir in the kirsch, then remove from the heat.

To make the crumble topping, put the flour and cinnamon in a bowl, then rub in the butter with your fingertips until the mixture resembles fine breadcrumbs. Now stir in 4 tablespoons of the raw brown sugar and the chopped cashews.

When the peaches are cool enough to handle (use a knife and fork if necessary), gently remove and discard the skins. Cut the peach flesh into bite-size chunks and arrange evenly in the bottom of an ovenproof saucepan. Pour over the syrup, then lightly sprinkle over the crumble mixture in an even layer. Do not press the crumble into the syrup or it will become mushy. Sprinkle over the remaining raw brown sugar and bake in the preheated oven for 25–30 minutes, or until the crumble topping is golden brown. Remove from the oven and serve with vanilla- or peach-flavored ice cream.

serves 4

12 oz/350 g cherries, pitted

½ tsp allspice

3 tbsp raw brown sugar

3 tbsp cherry brandy

vanilla ice cream, to serve

crumble topping

1¼ cups all-purpose flour

½ tsp allspice

¼ cup raw brown sugar, plus extra for sprinkling

½ cup unsalted butter, melted

1¾ oz/50 g almonds, chopped

spiced cherry crumble

Preheat the oven to 375°F/190°C. To make the filling, put the cherries, allspice, sugar, and cherry brandy into a saucepan and stir gently over low heat for 3 minutes. Transfer the cherries and juices to an ovenproof pan.

To make the crumble topping, put the flour, allspice, and sugar in a large bowl, then mix in half the melted butter. Stir in the chopped nuts, then quickly mix in the remaining butter until crumbly. Carefully arrange the crumble over the cherries in an even layer—keep your touch light or the crumble will sink into the filling and go mushy. Scatter a little more sugar over the top, then transfer to the preheated oven and bake for 15–20 minutes, or until the crumble topping is golden brown.

Remove from the oven and serve with vanilla ice cream.

serves 4

1 lb 12 oz/800 g ripe but firm
gooseberries

2 tbsp honey

¼ cup superfine sugar,
or to taste

vanilla ice cream, to serve

cobbler topping

1½ cups self-rising flour, plus
extra for dusting

pinch of salt

½ tsp mixed spice

3 tbsp butter

2 tbsp superfine sugar

1 egg, beaten

5 tbsp milk, plus extra
for glazing

gooseberry cobbler with honey & mixed spice

Preheat the oven to 400°F/200°C. Top and tail the gooseberries, arrange them evenly in the bottom of an ovenproof saucepan, then sprinkle over the honey and sugar and cook in the preheated oven for 5–10 minutes until heated through.

To make the cobbler topping, sift the flour, salt, and mixed spice into a large mixing bowl. Rub in the butter with your fingertips until the mixture resembles fine breadcrumbs, then mix in the sugar, followed by the beaten egg. Stir in enough of the milk to make a smooth dough. Transfer to a clean, lightly floured board, knead lightly, then roll out to a thickness of about $^1/_2$ inch/1 cm. Cut out circles using a 2-inch/5-cm cookie cutter. Arrange the dough circles over the gooseberries, then brush the tops with a little milk.

Bake in the preheated oven for 25–30 minutes, or until the cobbler topping has risen and is lightly golden. Remove from the oven and serve with vanilla ice cream.

serves 4

2 ripe mangoes, pitted and cut into fairly thick slices

9 oz/250 g blueberries

½ tsp grated nutmeg

1 tbsp lime juice

¼ cup superfine sugar, or to taste

stirring custard or heavy cream, to serve

cobbler topping

1½ cups self-rising flour, plus extra for dusting

pinch of salt

½ tsp cinnamon

3 tbsp butter

2 tbsp superfine sugar

3 tbsp dried blueberries (optional)

1 egg, beaten

5 tbsp milk, plus extra for glazing

spiced mango & blueberry cobbler

Preheat the oven to 400°F/200°C. Put the mangoes and blueberries in the bottom of an ovenproof saucepan, then sprinkle over the nutmeg, lime juice, and superfine sugar and cook in the preheated oven for 5–10 minutes until heated through.

To make the cobbler topping, sift the flour, salt, and cinnamon into a large mixing bowl. Rub in the butter with your fingertips until the mixture resembles fine breadcrumbs, then mix in the sugar, and the dried blueberries, if using. Add the beaten egg, then stir in enough of the milk to make a smooth dough. Transfer to a clean, lightly floured board, knead lightly, then roll out to a thickness of about ½ inch/1 cm. Cut out circles using a 2-inch/5-cm cookie cutter. Arrange the dough circles over the fruit, then brush the tops with a little milk.

Bake in the preheated oven for 25–30 minutes, or until the cobbler topping has risen and is lightly golden. Remove from the oven and serve with stirring custard or heavy cream.

serves 4

1 large onion, peeled and sliced

2 zucchini, sliced

3 oz/85 g mushrooms, sliced

2 large carrots, coarsely chopped

8 oz/225 g canned black-eyed peas, rinsed and drained

6 oz/175 g canned cannellini beans, rinsed and drained

14 oz/400 g canned tomatoes

1 tsp mild chili powder

salt and pepper

cobbler topping

1¼ cups self-rising flour, plus extra for dusting

2 level tsp baking powder

½ tsp paprika

3 tbsp butter

4–5 tbsp milk

salt

spicy vegetable cobbler

Preheat the oven to 400°F/200°C. Put the onion, zucchini, mushrooms, carrots, black-eyed peas, cannellini beans, and canned tomatoes in an ovenproof casserole. Sprinkle over the chili powder and season to taste with salt and pepper. Transfer to the preheated oven and bake for 15 minutes.

Meanwhile, to make the cobbler topping, sift the flour, baking powder, paprika, and a pinch of salt into a large mixing bowl. Rub in the butter until the mixture resembles fine breadcrumbs, then stir in enough of the milk to make a smooth dough. Transfer to a clean, lightly floured board, knead lightly, then roll out to a thickness of about ½ inch/1 cm. Cut out circles using a 2-inch/5-cm cookie cutter.

Remove the casserole from the oven, arrange the dough circles over the top, then return to the oven and bake for 30 minutes, or until the cobbler topping has risen and is lightly golden. Remove from the oven and serve hot.

serves 4

2 tbsp all-purpose flour

2 lb/900 g braising beef, cut
into bite-size chunks

2 tbsp chili oil or olive oil

1 large onion, peeled and
sliced

1 garlic clove, crushed

1 small red chile, deseeded
and chopped

1 zucchini, sliced

1 red bell pepper, seeded and
cut into small chunks

5 1/2 oz/150 g mushrooms,
sliced

1 tbsp tomato paste

2 cups red wine

1 cup beef stock or vegetable
stock

1 bay leaf

salt and pepper

cobbler topping

1 1/4 cups self-rising flour,
plus extra for dusting

2 level tsp baking powder

pinch of cayenne pepper

3 tbsp butter

4–5 tbsp milk

salt

beef cobbler with chile

Preheat the oven to 325°F/160°C. Put the flour in a bowl, season with salt
and pepper, then add the beef chunks and toss in the flour to coat. Heat
half of the oil in a large flameproof casserole, add the beef, and cook,
stirring, until the meat has browned all over and is seared. Lift out with
a slotted spoon, transfer to a plate, and set aside.

Heat the remaining oil in the casserole, add the onion and garlic, and cook
over medium heat, stirring, for 2 minutes until softened. Add the chile,
zucchini, red bell pepper, and mushrooms and cook, stirring, for another
3 minutes.

Stir in the remaining seasoned flour and the tomato paste, then stir in the
red wine, scraping the bottom gently to deglaze the casserole. Pour in the
stock, add the bay leaf, then bring to a boil. Reduce the heat and cook over
low heat, stirring, until thickened. Return the beef to the saucepan, cover,
and bake in the preheated oven for 45 minutes.

Meanwhile, to make the cobbler topping, sift the flour, baking powder,
cayenne pepper, and a pinch of salt into a large mixing bowl. Rub in the
butter with your fingertips until the mixture resembles fine breadcrumbs,
then stir in enough of the milk to make a smooth dough. Transfer to a
clean, lightly floured board, knead lightly, then roll out to a thickness of
about 1/2 inch/1 cm. Cut out circles using a 2-inch/5-cm cookie cutter.

Remove the casserole from the oven, remove and discard the bay leaf, and
adjust the seasoning. Arrange the dough circles over the top, then return to
the oven and bake for another 30 minutes, or until the cobbler topping has
risen and is lightly golden. Remove from the oven and serve hot.